GROWING CRYSTALS

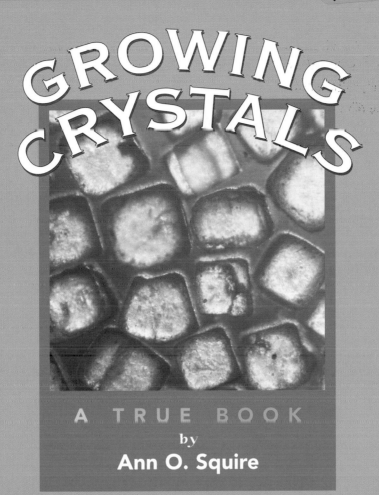

A TRUE BOOK

by

Ann O. Squire

Children's Press®

A Division of Scholastic Inc.

New York Toronto London Auckland Sydney
Mexico City New Delhi Hong Kong
Danbury, Connecticut

Emerald crystals

Reading and Content
Consultant
Jan Jenner

Author's Dedication
To my daughter, Emma

The photograph on the cover
shows selenite crystals. The
photograph on the title page
shows tiny salt crystals.

Squire, Ann.
  Growing crystals / by Ann O. Squire.
      p.   cm. – (True Books)
  Includes index.
  Summary: Introduction to growing crystals, discussing the different
types of crystals and how they are made.
    ISBN 0-516-22340-2 (lib. bdg.)   0-516-26984-4 (pbk.)
    1. Crystal growth—Juvenile literature. [1. Crystal growth. 2. Crystals]
I. Title. II. True book.
QD921 S63 2002
548'.5—dc21   2001005757

SCHOLASTIC and associated designs are trademarks and/or registered
trademarks of Scholastic Inc. CHILDREN'S PRESS, TRUE BOOKS, and
A TRUE BOOK and all associated designs are trademarks and/or
registered trademarks of Grolier Publishing Company, Inc.
16 17 18 19 20 R 12 11   62

Contents

Chandeliers, wineglasses, and diamonds all look like they are true crystals.

What Is a Crystal?

If someone asked you to describe a crystal, how would you reply? Maybe you would point to the sparkling chandelier hanging over your dining-room table, or to the delicate wineglasses your parents use on special occasions, or even to the diamond in your mom's engagement ring. All of these things are clear, and all sparkle and shine when the sunlight strikes them. But only one of them is really a crystal (you'll have to read Chapter 2 to find out which!). What's more, not all crystals are bright and shiny. Some are dark and rather dull. So what makes a crystal a crystal?

Calcite crystals have a square shape.

The first thing to know about crystals is that they are always solid, never liquid or gas. But these solids are not lumpy blobs, like rocks.

This quartz has long, rectangular crystals on top.

Instead, crystals come in regular, geometric shapes, with sharp, straight edges and smooth sides, or faces. Crystals can be shaped like cubes, diamonds, bricks, pyramids, six-sided bars, books, and even needles. They can be octahedrons (which look like two four-sided pyramids glued together), pyritohedrons (solids with twelve five-sided faces), and other shapes that are almost too complex to

Gypsum crystals are thin and spiky.

describe. Crystals can also have very complicated shapes that are a combination of several simpler shapes. A particular kind of crystal usually has the same shape. Salt crystals, for instance, are always cubes. Garnets, however, can also be shaped like cubes, or have twelve-faced or twenty-four-faced shapes.

Why do crystals always have such regular shapes? The answer can be found by peering

Scientists use special X-ray
machines to look inside crystals.

deep inside the crystal.
Scientists called crystallogra-
phers use X-rays to do this.
The X-rays show that the very
tiny particles (called atoms)

that make up the crystal are also arranged in a regular and orderly way. Each atom has its own position, and each is attached to its neighbors by either weak or strong forces,

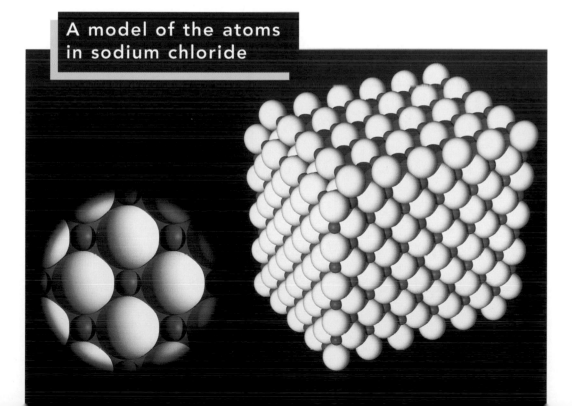

A model of the atoms in sodium chloride

called bonds. It is the regular arrangement of atoms on the inside that gives each crystal its very special shape on the outside. The strength of the bonds between the atoms determines the hardness of the crystal. It also determines how the crystal breaks. Crystals always break cleanly and smoothly along the line where the bonds between atoms are weakest.

Crystals Around the House

Now that you know a bit about crystals, let's go back to the chandelier, the wineglass, and the diamond. Which is the real crystal? X-rays of each object would reveal that only the diamond has a regular, geometric arrangement of atoms (in this

A diamond is a true crystal.

case, carbon atoms) on the inside. The chandelier and the wineglass are made of glass that has been cut to look like the faces of crystals. But an X-ray would show that the atoms in the glass are "all over the

Depending on their arrangement, carbon atoms may form diamonds, like in this model.

place." They are not arranged in a regular, orderly way. So while a diamond and a glass may look similar on the outside, they are very different on the inside. Only the diamond is a true crystal.

It's All in the Atoms

The arrangement of atoms and the bonds between them are very important to the finished crystal. Take the case of carbon. One arrangement of carbon atoms produces the eight-sided crystal we know as a diamond. A different arrangement of the same atoms produces graphite, which is used to make the "lead" in pencils. A diamond is the hardest mineral in existence, and graphite is one of the softest.

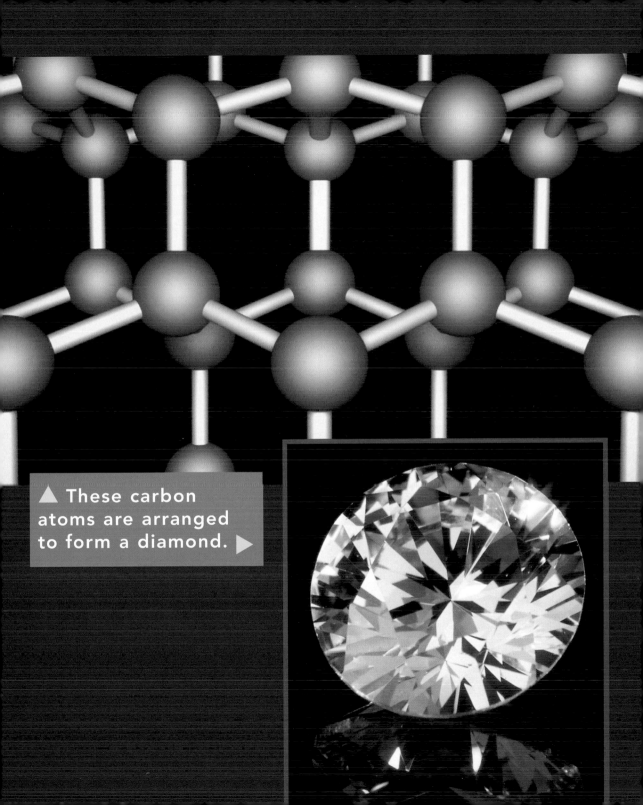

▲ These carbon atoms are arranged to form a diamond. ▶

Once you start looking, you can find crystals all around the house. It will help to have a magnifying glass, as most of the crystals you'll encounter are quite small.

Let's begin in the kitchen. Pour a few grains from the saltshaker onto a clean surface (a piece of dark construction paper works well). Hold the paper under a bright light and look at the salt grains with your magnifying glass. You'll

It is easiest to view salt cubes on a dark background.

Salt grains are tiny, perfect cubes.

see that each grain of salt is actually a tiny, perfect cube. If you were to crush one of the salt crystals and look at the pieces, you would see that the cube breaks into a number of even smaller cubes.

The sugar in your sugar bowl is also made up of crystals. Sugar crystals are not cubes, like salt, but look more like flattened rectangles. Right now there are

Ice crystals (above); Snowflakes are six-sided crystals (left).

probably some crystals of ice in your freezer, and if it's snowing outside, you might notice that each snowflake is actually a six-sided crystal, with longer, spiky crystals growing outward from it.

There are many more every-day objects in your home that are based on crystals. The aspirin and vitamin C in your bathroom are made of crystals, your watch may contain tiny crystals of ruby or quartz, and your telephone, TV, radio, and camera all depend on crystals to work. Even if you can't see them, crystals are everywhere!

How Crystals Are Formed

Crystals are created in three ways. One is through the slow cooling of molten (melted) material. When rock, metal, or another material is heated until it melts, the atoms inside it zip around rapidly. As the material begins to cool, the

The atoms inside melted rock move around very quickly.

atoms slow down. If the cooling process is slow enough, the atoms gradually stop moving and take their positions in the regular, orderly arrangement of a crystal. As the material gets cooler and cooler, the layers of the crystal build up. The more slowly the material cools, the larger the crystals will be. Gemstones such as emeralds, rubies, sapphires, and diamonds were all

Emeralds and rubies form
when heated material cools
slowly within the ground.

formed by the slow cooling
of minerals deep within the
ground.

Obsidian is created when the contents of a volcanic explosion cool.

When a melted material cools too quickly, the solid object that is formed is not a crystal. Obsidian, a shiny black glass, is created when volcanoes erupt. As the hot lava shoots into the air, it cools down very quickly. There is no time for the atoms to take their positions in a crystal structure. The cooling is so quick that the atoms in the lava are "frozen" into place.

Lava explodes from deep within Earth.

Crystals can also be created when a warm gas cools down. This is how snow is formed. When the air temperature drops below freezing, water droplets crystallize into tiny, six-sided shapes. As they fall to the ground, long, branching ice crystals sprout from the edges, creating larger crystals. Several crystals may clump together to create the fat, fluffy snowflakes you see in winter.

Snowflakes are formed when the air temperature drops below freezing and water droplets crystallize.

The last way that crystals can form is when a liquid that contains dissolved minerals evaporates very slowly. Evaporation is the process through which a liquid is transformed into a gas. The salt crystals that you use every day may have been created that way. In the next chapter, you will learn how to use evaporation to make crystals of your own.

Growing Crystals

Growing your own crystals at home is fun, and surprisingly easy. One of the simplest crystals to grow is halite, which is the official name for common table salt. Halite is made up of sodium and chlorine atoms bonded together in cube-shaped crystals.

When you dissolve table salt in water, the sodium and chlorine atoms separate and float around on their own, surrounded by shells of water molecules. When the water evaporates, the atoms come together again as halite crystals.

To grow your own, mix one teaspoon of salt with six teaspoons of water. Stir until the mixture becomes clear, then

Mix one teaspoon of salt with six teaspoons of water.

pour it into a shallow pan and leave it in a warm, dry place. After a day or so, the water will evaporate, leaving fairly big white cubes of halite. You can crush some of the large cubes and look at them through your magnifying glass to see the tiny cubes they have become.

Sugar will also form large crystals. In fact, if you've ever had rock candy, you have eaten sugar crystals without

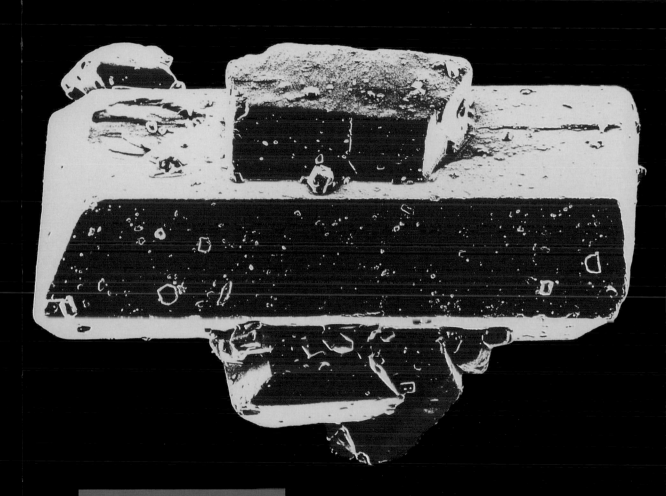

Close-up of a large
sugar cane crystal

even knowing it. To make sugar crystals, have an adult heat about 2/3 of a cup of water until it begins to boil. Turn off the heat, and stir in confectioner's sugar a tablespoon at a time, until no more will dissolve. Pour the syrup into a clean jar. Next, take a thin cotton string and tie one end of it to a paper clip and the other end to the middle of a pencil. Drop the paper clip into the syrup and rest the pencil across the top of the jar, so that the string hangs down into the sugar mixture. The paper clip should be just above the bottom of the jar, so you may need to wrap the string around the pencil to shorten it.

Put the jar in a warm, dry place and let it sit undisturbed. After a few days, you should see tiny crystals beginning to form on the string. In the next couple of days, the crystals will grow larger. After about a week, remove the crystals from the syrup. How big are they? How do their shapes compare to the shapes of the salt crystals you grew? Once you've examined and admired them, feel free

Rock candy is the delicious product of sugar and water.

to remove some crystals and eat the results of your experiment!

To Find Out More

Here are some additional resources to help you learn more about crystals:

 **Books**

Farndon, John. **Collecting Rocks and Crystals.** Sterling Publications, 2000.

Hall, Cathy. **DK Handbooks: Gemstones.** DK Publishing, 1994.

Stangl, Jean. **Crystals and Crystal Gardens You Can Grow.** Franklin Watts, 1992.

Symes, R.F. **Eyewitness: Crystals and Gems.** DK Publishing, 2000.

Organizations and Online Sites

Collecting Rocks and Minerals

kidscollecting.miningco. com/library/weekly/ aa100700a.htm

Here's more information about rocks and crystals and how to collect them.

Crystal Creations

netra.exploratrium.edu/ science_explorer/crystals. html

Learn how to grow spikes of crystals in the sun.

Enchanted Rocks— Minerals, Crystals, and Polished Stones

www.enchantedrocks.com/ Experiments.html

More information on crystals, mineral guides, experiments, and a geology timeline.

Snow and Blizzards

www.nearctica.com/ geology/storms/snow.htm

Find out more about snow crystals.

Important Words

atom the smallest part of an element that can exist

bonds the weak or strong forces that hold atoms together in a crystalline structure

crystal a solid mineral with a geometric shape, straight edges, and smooth faces. All crystals are made up of atoms that are arranged in a regular, orderly way

crystallographer a scientist who studies crystals

evaporation the process through which water changes from a liquid into a gas, called water vapor

molten melted

Index

(**Boldface** page numbers indicate illustrations.)

Meet the Author

Ann O. Squire has a Ph.D. in animal behavior. Before becoming a writer, she studied African electric fish, rats, and other animals. Dr. Squire has written many books on animals, animal behavior, and other natural science topics. Her most recent books for Children's Press include *Animals of the Sea and Shore, African Animals, Animal Babies,* and *Animal Homes.* She lives with her children, Emma and Evan, in Bedford, New York.